SA... ...TS

ELEPHANT
DREAMS

SANDWICH POETS

ELEPHANT DREAMS

IAN McMILLAN
DAVID HARMER
and
PAUL COOKSON

Illustrated by
Lucy Maddison

MACMILLAN CHILDREN'S BOOKS

First published 1998 by
Macmillan Children's Books
a division of Macmillan Publishers Ltd
25 Eccleston Place London SW1W 9NF
Basingstoke and Oxford
www.macmillan.co.uk

Associated companies throughout the world

ISBN 0330 35 338 1

5 7 9 8 6 4

A CIP catalogue record for this book is available from the British Library.

Typeset by Macmillan Children's Books
Printed by Mackays of Chatham plc, Chatham, Kent

CONTENTS

Ian McMillan

David Harmer

Paul Cookson

Ian McMillan

Ian was born in 1956, and has been a freelance writer, broadcaster and performer since 1981. He is currently poet in residence at Barnsley Football Club and is Yorkshire TV's investigative poet.

School in the Holidays

Down the corridors
nothing happens.

In the window's light
nobody moves.

The race is over,
the engine is cooling

and the school is like a driver
removing his gloves.

This Little Poem

This little poem has five lines
and five words on every line.
I wrote it out five times
between five o'clock and five past nine
using five different pencils every time
and this little poem tells lies.

Ten Things Found in a Wizard's Pocket

A dark night.
Some words that nobody could ever spell.
A glass of water full to the top.
A large elephant.
A vest made from spiders' webs.
A handkerchief the size of a car park.
A bill from the wand shop.
A bucket full of stars and planets, to mix with the dark night.
A bag of magic mints you can suck for ever.
A snoring rabbit.

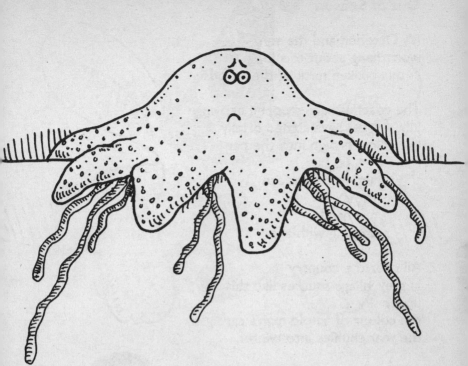

Ten Things Found in a Shipwrecked Sailor's Pocket

A litre of sea.
An unhappy jellyfish.
A small piece of a lifeboat.
A pencil wrapped around with seaweed.
A soaking feather.
The first page of a book called *Swimming is Easy*.
A folded chart showing dangerous rocks.
A photograph of a little girl in a red dress.
A gold coin.
A letter from a mermaid.

Out of Season

It's October, and the sun
won't hang about too long
in this broken neck of the woods.

The coaches have stopped arriving.
July, August have sizzled briefly
like chips thrown into the pan

    and in the breeze
    the trees
    are hands
    shaking with age.

All over the country
in grey village squares like this
under sky
the colour of an old man's cardigan
the year shuffles into winter,

and the village's six children
if they lived near the sea
would walk by the sea.

Instead they walk
from the phone box
to the bus stop

and from the phone box
to the fish and chip caravan.

This is a postcard
no one sends home. Nobody
wishes they were here.

From the phone box
you can see the bus stop
and little else

and in the breeze
the trees
are hands
shaking with age.

Can't be Bothered to Think of a Title

When they make slouching in the chair
an Olympic sport
I'll be there.

When they give out a cup
for refusing to get up
I'll win it every year.

When they hand out the gold
for sitting by the fire
I'll leave the others in the cold,

and when I'm asked to sign my name
in the Apathetic Hall of Fame
I won't go.

8

Going to Sleep

Going to sleep is a funny thing,
I lie in bed and I'm yawning
and Dad is reading a story and then . . .

suddenly it's morning!

Elephant Dreams

1.

I'm so small
I can crawl
under a leaf

and I can look
into the world
from underneath

2.

There's a huge grey cloud in the sky.
It's me.
I float down onto a sycamore
tree.
I burst like a bag and the rain falls
out.
I swim in my rain like a big grey
trout.

3.

My
long
trunk
goes
round
the
world
twice!

4.

I am the last elephant
and I stare into the sun
as it falls into the night
and in the fading light
I know my race is run.
I am the last elephant.

5.

I can't move.
People are staring at me.

I can't move.
People are walking by.

I can't move.
Children are pointing at me.

I can't move.
Is this where you go when you die?

Spot the Hidden Part of a Loaf

Look carefully
because within this poem
is hiddenCRUST
the name of a part
of a loaf.

ThisCRUST
part of a loaf
is just in the poem
for a laugh.

SomebodyCRUST said
to me
'I bet you can't hide
part of a loaf
in a poem.'

CRUST

Have you spotted it yet?
Have you spotted it yet?

Coded Nursery Rhymes

Note: The code increases in difficulty, but here's a clue; it's a bit fishy. See if you can crack it. Good luck!

I.   AN EASY ONE

Jack and Jill went up the fish
to fetch a pail of water.
Jack fell down and broke his fish
and Fish came tumbling after.

TRA LA LA

2.   A HARDER ONE

Little Fish Horner
sat fish a fish
eating a Christmas fish.
He fish in his fish
and fish fish fish plum
and said
'Fish Fish Fish Fish Fish I.'

3.   A VERY HARD ONE

Fish Fish
fish fish fish wall.
Fish Fish
fish fish great fish.
Fish fish fish fish
and fish fish fish fish
fish fish fish fish again.

Goodnight Stephen

At first it was the smell,
the smell of a torch
drifting up like mist through the field.

Then it was the sound,
the sound of a torch,
a noise like a torchbeam unzipping the tent.

Now it's the weight,
the weight of a torchbeam
across the sleeping bag onto my face.

I must be asleep
but I think I'm waking up.

The stink of the torchbeam
smells awful, smells scary.
A torchbeam feels spiky.

The taste of the torchbeam
tastes rotten, tastes fishy.
A torchbeam feels chilly.

I think I'm waking up.
I can't be asleep.

Then it was the smell,
the smell of a pipe
through the flap of the tent,

and it was the sound,
the sound of my dad
saying 'Just checking. Goodnight.'

Now it's the weight, the weight of my head
on the pillow as darkness returns.

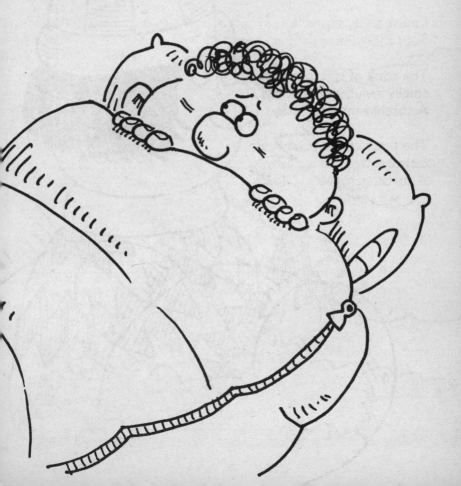

The Fog and Me

It was so foggy today
I couldn't see my hand
in front of my face.

I know because I waved at myself
and I didn't wave back.

No Bread

I wish I'd made a list
I forgot to get the bread.
If I forget it again
I'll be dead.

We had blank and butter pudding,
beans on zip.
Boiled egg with deserters,
no chip butty: just chip.

NO BREAD!

I wish I'd made a list
I forgot to get the bread.
My mam got the empty bread bin
and wrapped it round my head.

Our jam sarnies were just jam
floating on the air.
We spread butter on the table
cos the bread wasn't there.

My mam says if I run away
she knows I won't be missed,
not like the bread was . . .
I wish I'd made a list!

17

Homework

I love my school so very much
that I'm taking it home
bit by bit in my bag.

My mother says it's stealing
but I don't think it's stealing,
it's really just collecting.

I've got three bricks
and a desk so far.

The bricks were easy
but the desk was hard.

Another Christmas Present from Auntie Mabel

What a silly present.
I can't understand it.

I don't eat seaweed because it tastes foul.
I don't wear seaweed because it looks awful.
I don't take seaweed for walks because it slips off the lead.
I don't watch videos on seaweed because they get smelly.
I don't play football with seaweed because it doesn't bounce.

I can't understand it.
What a silly present.

Fred

I'm Fred, the school caretaker
without a head,
look at me
I'm Fred, the school caretaker
without a head.

My head fell off in bed the other night,
I looked at my wife and she died of fright,

I'm Fred, the school caretaker
without a head.

When I go to the pub me mates say flippin 'eck
cos I carry the beer on top of me neck.

I'm Fred, the school caretaker
without a head.

Some vandals came to school and they seemed pretty rough
but I just had to look at them, that was enough.

I'm Fred, the school caretaker
without a head.

The Dragon's Birthday Party

It's the dragon's birthday party,
he's ten years old today.
'Come and do your special trick,'
I heard his mother say.

We crowded round the table,
we pushed and shoved to see
as someone brought the cake mix in
and the dragon laughed with glee.

It was just a bowl with flour in
and eggs and milk and that
with ten blue candles round the top
in the shape of Postman Pat.

The dragon took a big deep breath
stood up to his full size
and blew a blast of smoke and flame
that made us shut our eyes.

We felt the air grow hotter
we knew the taste of fear.
I felt a spark fly through the air
and land on my left ear.

But when we looked,
make no mistake:
the candles were lit
and the cake was baked.

Names of Scottish Islands to be Shouted in a Bus Queue when you're Feeling Bored.

Yell!
Muck!
Eigg!
Rhum!
Unst!
Hoy!
Foula!
Coll!
Canna!
Barra!
Gigha!
Jura!
Pabay!
Raasay!
Skye!

Time Slips Backwards in my Auntie's House

When we sat down to tea
it was twenty past three.

When the cakes had all gone
it was quarter to one.

When I got up to go
I was caught in the flow;

I felt myself yawn,
day had melted to dawn,

Time had sprung a big leak!
I'd slipped into last week!

Strange Books on a High Shelf

My Journey to the Centre of the Sun: 222 pages, some smoking.

The New No-eat Diet: 333 pages, some chewed.

The Great Treacle Flood of 1836: 444 pages, some sticky.

How to Turn a Book into a Clock: 444 pages, some ticky.

Cooking with Paper and Ink: 333 pages, some stewed.

The Book of Exaggerations: 2,222,222 pages, I'm joking!

David Harmer

David Harmer was born in 1952. He lives and works in Doncaster where he is a primary school headmaster. David has been writing stories and poems for children and adults for many years. He has appeared several times on radio and television, most recently on the BBC's poetry programme *Wham Bam Strawberry Jam*.

Flight from Planet Earth

Landing here because we had to
the fuel gone and the computers broken
we crashed into a bank of sand
let the dust die down
then climbed out of our rocket.

We were surrounded by eyes
along the rim of the distant mountains
in the desert at our feet,
it was worse at night
when they glowed like fires
staring at us without blinking.

Time has passed
we live in the wreck of our spacecraft
eat what is left of our stores
drink rainwater
sometimes we go out looking for food,
the creatures always force us back
make us afraid,
we are the aliens here
and they don't like us.

Phew!

Something's outside our tent
A slithery, snuffling noise
I don't know what it is
But I know that it eats boys.

Something's outside our tent
I bet it's big and hairy
With chomping jaws and bulging eyes
Looking very scary.

Something's outside our tent
It's grunting and it's near
Sounds like it could freeze my blood
Keep it out of here!

Something's outside our tent
I hope it's gone by morning.
Wait a tick, it's next door's tent
It's only Darren snoring!

A Televised Surprise

Imagine our delight
Consternation and surprise
Our teacher on *Come Dancing*
Right before our eyes.

She wore a dress of sequins
That glittered like a flight
Of silent, silver snowflakes
On a winter's night.

She really looked fantastic
No one could ignore
The magic of her dancing
Across the ballroom floor.

Her partner, tall and smart
Only saw him from the back,
Oily hair slicked down short
His suit and shoes were black.

He whirled and twirled her round
As the music got much faster
And then he faced the camera
It was our headmaster!

They seemed to dance for ever
Until it wasn't fun
And then the competition stopped
The pair of them had won.

On a Blue Day

On a blue day
when the brown heat
scorches the grass
and stings my legs with sweat

I go running like a fool
up the hill towards the trees
and my heart beats loudly
like a kettle boiling dry.

I need a bucket the size of the sky
filled with cool, cascading water.

At evening
the cool air rubs my back
I listen to the bees
working for their honey

and the sunset pours light
over my head like a waterfall.

There's a Monster in the Garden

If the water in your fishpond fizzes and foams
And there's giant teeth marks on the plastic gnomes
You've found huge claw prints in the flower bed
And just caught sight of a two-horned head
Put a stick in your front lawn with a piece of card on
Look out everybody – there's a monster in the garden!

You haven't seen the dustman for several weeks
Haven't seen the gasman who was looking for leaks
Haven't seen the paper-girl, postman or plumber
Haven't seen the window cleaner since last summer
Don't mean to be nosy, I do beg your pardon
Look out everybody – there's a monster in the garden!

One dark night it will move in downstairs
Start living in the kitchen, take you unawares
Frighten you, bite on you, with howls and roars
It will crash about, smash about, push you out of doors
In the cold and snow the ice and rain will harden
Look out everybody – there's a monster in the garden!

Now listen to me, neighbour, all of this is true
It happened next door, now it's happening to you.
There's something nasty on the compost heap
Spends all day there curled up asleep
You don't want your bones crunched or jarred on
Look out everybody – there's a monster in the garden!

My Mum's put me on the Transfer List

On Offer:
one nippy striker, ten years old
has scored seven goals this season
has nifty footwork and a big smile
knows how to dive in the penalty box
can get filthy and muddy within two minutes
guaranteed to wreck his kit each week
this is a FREE TRANSFER
but he comes with running expenses
weeks of washing shirts and shorts
socks and vests, a pair of trainers
needs to scoff huge amounts
of chips and burgers, beans and apples
pop and cola, crisps and oranges
endless packets of chewing gum.
This offer open until the end of the season
I'll have him back then
at least until the cricket starts.
Any takers?

What the Mountains Do

What the mountains do is
roar silent warnings over
huge brown and heather-covered spaces

or fill up valleys with dark green laughter

before resting their stone-cropped heads
in sunlight.

Alone

The sun has been punctured
sagged out of sight behind the clouds.

I'm alone in the house
watching the moon lay long, cold fingers

Onto the curtains and through the glass
in the creaking windows.

If the footsteps outside come up the path
I'm going to hide under my bed.

If the hand I can hear tapping a key
turns the lock and opens the door

I'm going to scamper along the landing
shove the bolt tight on the bathroom door.

If the voice I can hear breathing hard
hisses and whispers up the stairs

I'm going to scramble down the drainpipe
and run for cover in the back garden.

Monsters are clever, these two for example
set their trap by calling my name

In the exact voice of my dad home from work
and of my mum back from the shops.

But I know their tricks, they won't catch me
although I suppose not many monsters

Bang and kick on the bathroom door
yelling 'Why at eleven years of age

Do we still have to go through this nonsense each time one of us nips to the shops?'

Perhaps I've got it wrong again.

Will it go to a Replay?

Last night's cup-tie
Everton and Sheffield United
was so exciting, really tough.

Two teams battled it out
through the rain and mud
as goal after goal
thudded into the net.

The crowd went wild
just loved
every nail-biting moment.

Four—four
with five minutes left
of extra time
both teams down to nine men
and the tension tightening.

In those dying minutes
both sides
cleared their goal lines
with desperate headers.

Everton missed a penalty
United missed an open goal.

With seconds to go
a replay at Bramall Lane
seemed certain, until

Everton had to go in for her tea
and Sheffield United went to the shops
for his mum.

The Best Bit About a School Trip

I've been to the place
where the Vikings once lived
it must have been cold.

I've been to the farm, seen horses
rare pigs and multi-coloured sheep
it was very smelly.

I've been to the seaside
collected seaweed, paddled in rockpools
got my jeans soaking wet.

I've dressed up as a Saxon
a Roman soldier and a Tudor king
felt very important.

But the very best bit
is eating your sandwiches, swapping your crisps
for your mate's biscuits.

Swigging your pop
stuffing your face with your mum's best cake
and too much chocolate.

Piling into the shop
buying pencils, erasers and notebooks
spending your money.

I'm an expert at this
four years in Junior School
has taught me a lot.

The Thing I Like Best About School Dinners

The thing I like best
about school dinners
is the sticky bit
at the top of the apple crumble
just where the apple juice and custard

Has dripped and dribbled
slithered and slunk
poured and percolated
soaked and saturated

Into one big gooey lump
that I can push into my mouth
like cement into a mixer.

It clogs up my tastebuds
with sugar-sweet concrete
until I think
that the sticky-sloppy-sludge
will make me clap my hands
with the wonderful slurp of it.

Until I feel
I can't take any more
of the chewy-chunky-glutinous-gunge
and my head will explode
with the marvellous splodge of it.

Until that is
I take the next spoonful
close my eyes
dredge back the gluey
throat-bunging slob and sweet glob of it.

And put up my hand for more.

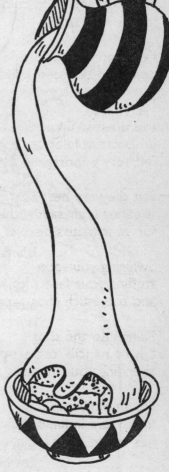

It's Behind You

I don't want to scare you
But just behind you
Is a . . .

No! Don't look!
Just act calmly
As if it wasn't there.

Like I said
Can you hear me if I whisper?
Just behind you
Is a . . .

NO! DON'T LOOK!
Just keep on reading
Don't turn round, believe me
It isn't worth it.

If you could see
what I can see standing there
You'd understand.

It's probably one
Of the harmless sort
Although with that mouth
Not to mention the teeth
And all that blood
Dripping down its chin
I wouldn't like to say.

DON'T TURN ROUND!
Listen
It's trying to speak
I think it wants to be friends.

Oh I see, it doesn't, never mind
You'd better leave just in case
I expect you'll escape
If you don't look round.

Oh what a shame!
I thought you'd make it
To the door. Hard luck.
I still think it means no harm.
I expect it eats all its friends.

Alien Exchange

WEIRD!

We've got an alien at our school
he's on an exchange trip
I'd quite fancy him
if he wasn't so weird looking.
Just one head
only two legs
and no feelers at all
he hasn't got claws on the end of his hands
and he's only got – don't laugh – two eyes.

Can you believe that?
When we first saw him we fell about
but as our teacher says
we must be thoughtful and respect all visitors
to our galaxy
even if they have got only one feeding system
a breathing tube that is much too small
and horrid furry stuff on their head.

Next month my sister and I
are visiting his planet on the exchange.
It's got a funny name, Earth.
We've got to stay two weeks
our teacher says we must be careful
not to tread on the Earthlings by mistake
and always, always be polite
to raise our wings in greeting
and to put rubber tips on our sharpest horns.
I'm not looking forward to it much
the food looks awful
and the sea's dirty, not to mention the air.

Still, it'll make a change from boring old school and perhaps some alien
will quite fancy me!

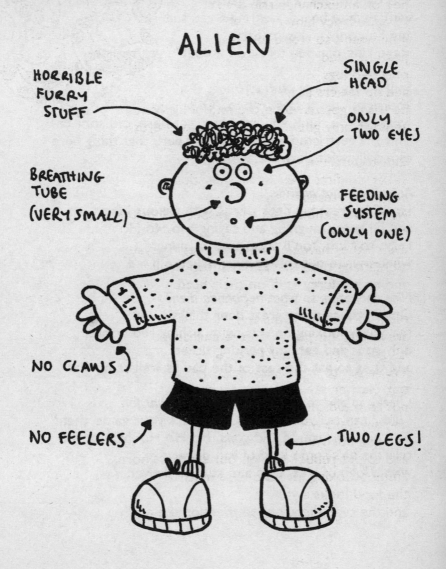

ALIEN

HORRIBLE FURRY STUFF

SINGLE HEAD

ONLY TWO EYES

BREATHING TUBE (VERY SMALL)

FEEDING SYSTEM (ONLY ONE)

NO CLAWS

NO FEELERS

TWO LEGS!

Two Traffic Wardens Talking on Christmas Eve

Nabbed any good ones yet?
Too right I have, a big fat geezer
with a white beard, wearing a red suit
and he's only trying to park
some kind of open truck on a double yellow line.

So you says to him push off?
Too right I did, I says to him, 'Oi
what do you think you are playing at here, old son? Eh?
This is a restricted zone, you can't park that thing here
especially with all those animals.'

Animals? What animals?
Horrible great big deer things with vicious horns
and he keeps laughing and saying 'Ho Ho Ho'
I says to him, 'You'll soon stop laughing
when I write out this parking ticket, old lad.'

Nice one, Stan, so what happened then?
One of those nasty great deer things
really ugly looking he was, with a shiny red hooter
only goes and eats my parking ticket
and tries to eat the rest of the pad as well as my hat.

Cheeky so and so, I hope you told him what for.
I did, I can tell you, I says 'Oi! What's your game then?'
And he turns round and goes 'Ho Ho Ho' back at me
tells me he's some kind of van driver
with a load of kids' toys and stuff to deliver.

So what? A double yellow line's a double yellow line.
Exactly, I soon told him, silly old fool
looked him straight in the eye and wrote out a ticket
on the back of a shopping list I had handy
'Who do you think you are?' I said, 'Father Christmas?'

The Elephant's Dictionary

Elegant:
What elephants always are
Especially at dinner.

Elevator:
How elephants go upstairs.

Elocution:
Polite trumpetings.

Elicopter:
Used by the elephant Flying Squad.

Elevision:
Home entertainment for the elephant
(also known as ellytelly).

Elescope:
A long-sighted elephant.

Elepathic:
a far-sighted elephant.

Elephone:
For trunk calls.

ELLO

Elementary:
Infants school for tiny tuskers.

Elegy:
Sad elephant's song.

Elements:
Rough weather for crossing the Alps.

Eletosis:
Bad breath on an elephant's tongue.

Elligator:
A snappy dresser amongst the pachyderms.

Lost in Space

When the spaceship first landed
nose down in Dad's prize vegetables
I wasn't expecting the pilot
to be a large blue blob with seven heads
the size and shape of rugby balls
and a toothy grin on his fourteen mouths.

'Is this Space Base Six?' he asked.
'No,' I said, 'it's our back garden, number fifty-two.'
'Oh,' he said, 'are you sure?'
and took from his silver overalls
a shiny book of maps.

There were routes round all the galaxies
ways to the stars through deepest space
maps to planets I'd never heard of
maps to comets, maps to moons
and short cuts to the sun.

'Of course,' he said, 'silly me,
I turned right, not left, at Venus,
easily done, goodbye.'
He shook his heads, climbed inside,
the spaceship roared into the sky
and in a shower of leeks and cabbages
disappeared for ever.

Harry Hobgoblin's Superstore

You want a gryphon's feather
Or a spell to change the weather?
A pixilating potion
To help you fly an ocean?
Some special brew of magic
To supercharge your broomstick?
Witches, wizards, why not pop
Into Harry's one-stop shop?

Tins of powdered dragon's teeth
Bottled beetles, newts.
Freeze-dried cobwebs, cats and rats
Screaming mandrake roots.
Lizard skins, stirred widdershins
A giant's big toe nail
Second-hand spells used only once
New ones that can't fail.
Spells to grow some donkey's ears
On the teacher no one likes
Spells to make you good at sums
Spells to find lost bikes.

Spells that grow and stretch and shrink
Spells that make your best friend stink
Sacks of spells stacked on my shelves
Come on in, see for yourselves.
Magic prices, bargains galore
At Harry Hobgoblin's Superstore.

The Lone Teacher

We've got a new teacher
he wears a mask
and a big wide hat.

He comes to school
on a silver horse
and rides around the field
all day.

Sometimes he says
'Have you seen Toronto?'

We tell him
we haven't been to Canada
but is it near
the Panama Canal
we did that in geography
last term.

At four o'clock
he rides off into the sunset
and comes back the next morning
in a cloud of dust.

We wonder if
he will ever come and teach us Maths
like he said he would
when he first arrived.

Perhaps then he'll tell us his name
not keep it a secret
because my dad always asks me
'Who is that man?'

Barry's Budgie . . . Beware!

Dave's got a dog the size of a lion
Half-wolf, half-mad, frothing with venom
It chews up policemen and then spits them out
But it's nothing to the bird I'm talking about.

Claire's got a cat as wild as a cheetah
Scratching and hissing, draws blood by the litre
Jumps high walls and hedges, fights wolves on its own
But there's one tough budgie it leaves well alone.

Murray my eel has teeth like a shark
Don't mess with Murray, he'll zap out a spark
But when Barry's budgie flies over the houses
Murray dims down his lights, blows his own fuses.

This budgie's fierce, a scar down its cheek
Tattoos on its wings, a knife in its beak
Squawks wicked words, does things scarcely legal
Someone should tell Barry, it's really an eagle.

Pasting Patsy's Pasty Posters

Petra Porter pastes in precincts
Patsy's pasty pasties posters
Patsy's posters for her pasties
and her tasty pastry pasta.

Patsy pays a pretty penny
For Petra's posters in the precincts
But Paula pastes her posters faster
Passes Petra, pasting past her.

So Patsy's pasting Paula's posters
paying pasty Paula plenty
for faster pasta poster pasting
pasting pasta posters faster.

Paul Cookson

Paul was born in 1961 and from an early age wanted
to either play football for Everton or guitar in Slade
(or preferably both). Since 1989 he has worked as a
writer and performed at thousands of venues.
Widely anthologized, he is also an editor and
occasional illustrator and his work has been featured
on national radio and television. He lives in Retford
with his wife Sally and son Sam.

Miss Smith's Mythical Bag

The curse of every class she'll see
No one knows its history
Its origin's a mystery
. . . Miss Smith's Mythical Bag.

Beyond our understanding
You dare not put your hand in
The bag that keeps expanding
. . . Miss Smith's Mythical Bag.

Broken chalk, a thousand pens with red ink that's congealed,
Forgotten fungus-covered bread with mouldy orange peel,
Lost car keys and headache pills, a Roman spear and shield,
Football cards and marbles, the goalposts from the field.

Where she goes it follows
All rippling lumps and hollows
The strangest things it swallows
. . . Miss Smith's Mythical Bag.

With a menacing unzipped grin it's
From the Outer Limits
There are black holes deep within it
. . . Miss Smith's Mythical Bag.

Crinkled tissues, Blu-tack balls, disfigured paperclips,
Sweets all covered up with fluff, dried up fibre-tips,
Lumps of powdered milk and coffee, last year's fish and chips,
From the Triangle in Bermuda — several missing ships.

Sometimes you hear it groan
Beyond the Twilight Zone
Make sure you're not alone
. . . with Miss Smith's Mythical Bag.

Shapeshifting, changing sizes,
The bag she never tidies,
It metamorphosizes
. . . Miss Smith's Mythical Bag.

More mysterious than Loch Ness, it's from the Fifth Dimension.
Stranger than an alien race beyond our comprehension.
Brooding with a strange intent that no one wants to mention
You'd better pay attention or you'll be in detention

With Miss Smith's mythical, metaphysical,
astronomical, gastronomical, anatomical,
clinical, cynical bag!

Sea Shoals See Shows on the Sea Bed

The salmon with a hat on was conducting with a baton
and it tried to tune the tuna fish by playing on its scales
the scales had all been flattened when the tuna fish was sat on
on purpose by a porpoise and a school of killer whales.
So the salmon with a hat on fiddled with his baton
while the angelfish got ready to play the tambourine.
Things began to happen when the salmon with a baton
was tapping out a pattern for the band of the marines.

There was a minnow on piano, a prawn with a horn,
an otter on guitar looking all forlorn.
A whale voice choir and a carp with a harp,
a belly-dancing jellyfish jiving with a shark.

The octaves on the octopus played the middle eight
but they couldn't keep in time with the skiffle-playing skate.
The plaice on the bass began to rock and roll
with the bloater in a boater and a Dover sole.

A clam on castanets, an eel on glockenspiel,
an oyster in a cloister singing with a seal.
The haddock had a headache from the deafening din
and the sword-dancing swordfish sliced off a fin.

A limpet on a trumpet, a flatfish on a flute,
the kipper fell asleep with King Canute.
Barracuda on a tuba sat upon a rock,
the electric eel gave everyone a shock.

The shrimp and the sturgeon, the stingray and the squid
sang a four-part harmony on the seabed.
The crab and the lobster gave their claws a flick,
kept everyone in time with their click click click . . .
kept everyone in time with their click click click . . .
kept everyone in time with their click click click.

Yes, the salmon with a hat on was tapping out a pattern
and things began to happen for the band of the marines.
It was an ocean of commotion of Atlantic proportion
the greatest show by schools of shoals that ever had
    been seen.

At the Back of the Cupboard Under the Stairs

At the back of the cupboard under the stairs
Deep in the shadows where nobody goes
Something clicks, sometimes whirs
Sometimes fast, sometimes slow
Sometimes high, sometimes low
Sometimes stop, sometimes go
Sometimes to, sometimes fro
Something stirs way down below.

At the back of the cupboard under the coats
Deep in the shadows something creaks
Something tries to clear its throat
Something strong, something sleek
Something long, something bleak
Something freaky and unique
Something let out once a week
Something wants something to eat.

At the back of the cupboard under the stairs
Deep in the shadows a creature roars
Something clicks, something whirs
Something just behind the door
Something waiting to explore
Something shaking on the floor
Something that you can't ignore
Something all of these and more.

A mouth that's wide and has no teeth
Devouring everything beneath.
Flexible neck, adjustable throat,
Dust-filled lungs that breathe out smoke.
A deathly monotone angry whine
A long thin tail that gets entwined
Tangling tables, strangling chairs
Roaming rooms, climbing stairs.

At the back of the cupboard under the stairs
Deep in the shadows where nobody goes
Something swallows dust and hairs
Nails from finger ends and toes
Sucked up scraps that decompose
Something lives, something grows
Something breathes, sucks and blows
Something waits to be exposed.

At the back of the cupboard under the stairs
. . . can you guess what is hiding there?

L-Plates on my Football Shirt

When I play football for the football team at school
no one takes me seriously, they think I'm just a fool.
My right boot's on my left foot, my left is on my right,
my socks are on my arms and my shorts are far too tight.

I have shin-pads on my chin just in case I'm fouled.
My shirt is full of holes, inside out and upside down.
The laces on my boots are nearly five miles long.
I need two weeks before each match so I can put them on.

They told me to play sweeper so I borrowed my mum's Hoover
and swept up their forward's shorts with a brilliant manoeuvre.
They asked about my shooting and how I could attack
so I got out my rifle but they made me put it back.

I told them that my dribbling was the best they'd get
then dribbled down their shirts and made them soaking wet.
They asked me to play winger, I said I couldn't fly.
'Well, mark your man instead', so I gave him two black eyes.

'Free-kick!' said the ref, so I did and watched him fall.
Nobody had told me that I had to kick the ball.
In view of this the referee gave the other team the kick.
I was told to build a wall but I couldn't find a brick.

In the end there's only two positions I can play:
left back right back in the changing rooms all day.
I'm only a beginner and someone could get hurt
so I don't have a number but an L-plate on my shirt.

An Elephant's Nose is Long I Suppose

An elephant's nose is long I suppose
to reach from her head to the tip of her toes
like an eye that smells out friends or foes
she uses it to say her hellos.
Hoover-like she sucks and blows
dust and sand she throws and throws
left to right and highs and lows
all of which just goes and shows
that an elephant knows how to use her nose.

Mum for a Day

Mum's ill in bed today
so I said I'd do the housework and look after things.
She told me it was really hard
but I said it'd be dead easy.
So . . .

I hoovered up the sink.

I dusted the cat.

I cooked my dad's shoes.

I washed up the carpet.

I fed all the ornaments and pictures.

Polished the steak and kidney pudding and chips.

Ironed all the letters and parcels.

Posted all the shirts and knickers.

Last of all . . .
I hung the budgie out on the washing line to dry.

It took me all day
but I got everything finished
and I was really tired.

I'm really glad Mum isn't ill every day
and do you know what?

So is the budgie.

The Toilet Seat has Teeth!

The bathroom has gone crazy
far beyond belief.
The sink is full of spiders
and the toilet seat has teeth!

The plughole in the bath
has a whirlpool underneath
that pulls you down feet first
and the toilet seat has teeth!

The toothpaste tube is purple
and makes your teeth fall out.
The toilet roll is nettles
and makes you scream and shout!

The towels have got bristles,
the bubble bath is glue,
the soap has turned to jelly
and it makes your skin bright blue.

The hot tap gushes forth
with a sludge that is bright pink.
The cold tap dribbles lumps
of green that block the sink.

The mirror's pulling faces
at everyone it can.
The shower's dripping marmalade
and blackcurrant jam.

The rubber ducks are breeding
and building their own nest
with shaving foam and tissues
in Grandad's stringy vest.

Shampoo is liquid dynamite,
there's petrol in the hairspray,
both will cure dandruff
when they blow your head away!

The bathroom has gone crazy
far beyond belief.
The sink is full of spiders
and the toilet seat has teeth!

The toilet seat has teeth! Ow!
The toilet seat has teeth! Ow!
The toilet seat has teeth! Ow!
The toilet seat has teeth! Ow!

Crunch! Slurp! Munch! Burp!
The toilet seat has teeth! Ow!
Don't – sit – on – it!
The toilet seat has . . .! Owwwww!

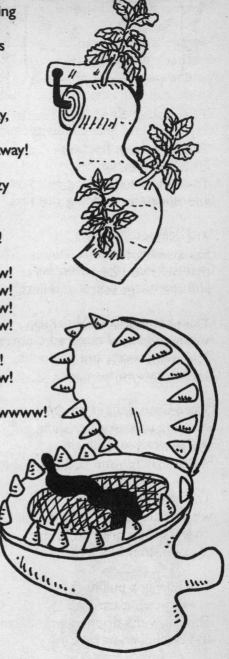

Mother is a Skinhead

Mother is a skinhead
Brother's heavy metal
Sister's into flower power
So we call her Petal.

Her boyfriend Shane likes techno
He's always on the rave
Grandma is a rapper Yo!
She repeats everything she says.
She repeats everything she says.

Dad dresses like Elvis
And greases back his hair.
Grandad likes the seventies
With platform boots and flares.

Uncle Frank's from Worksop
Ageing punk and tattered clothes
Chains and rings and padlocks
Join his ears to his nose.

Great-Gran dances go-go
She likes to shake her thing
The parrot's into jungle
The budgie's into swing.

Heavy rock at ninety-four years old
Affected Uncle Fred
His bathchair now does ninety-five
And he's got tattoos on his bald head.

Great-Aunt Clara's purple rinse
Shines out like a beacon
Now it's been replaced
With a pink and green mohican.

Auntie Rene, once removed,
From Italy, likes opera.
Uncle Clive likes to jive
But always lands on top of her.

Cousin Ray likes reggae
The baby sings the blues
The dog and cat like rock and roll
Both wear blue suede shoes.

Me . . . I don't like music
Can't sing or play guitar
So I've got the perfect qualities
To be a top pop star.

Rock around the clock, morning, noon and night
No one ever argues, no one ever fights
In tune with each other, a happy family
We'd like to teach the world to sing and live in harmony.

It

It hides inside your wardrobe
It hides beneath your bed
Sometimes Its eyes are yellow
And sometimes they are red.
It makes those spooky noises
That no one else can hear
And when you're fast asleep
It whispers in your ear.
It has ten thousand teeth
And eats your underwear

WHERE IS
IT?

And when you try and find your vest
It's never ever there.
It has a great big hairy nose
That's full of boils and spots
But doesn't seem to smell a thing
Because It eats your socks.
It hides your favourite toys
And breaks your favourite game
It colours on your favourite book
And you get all the blame.

It stops you doing homework
And switches on the telly.
It forces you to eat up all
The chocolate cake and jelly.
Sometimes It's very scary
And sometimes It is not
Sometimes It makes you very cold
And sometimes very hot.
When Mum and Dad and you
Are at the table to be fed
It makes a nasty noise and smell
And you get sent to bed.
It pinches all the sheets
In the middle of the night.
It makes the curtains flutter

And the bedroom door slam tight.
It taps upon your window
Its face is on the moon
It brings to life all shadows
That live inside your room.
It's the last thing you remember
Before you go to sleep.
It nearly bit your toes off
It nearly ate your feet
But always when you wake up
And feel the morning sun
It's never ever there
It's always always . . . gone.

Billy Doesn't Like School Really

Billy doesn't like school really.
It's not because he can't do the work
but because some of the other kids
don't seem to like him that much.

They call him names
and make up jokes about his mum.

Everyone laughs . . . except Billy.
Everyone laughs . . . except Billy.

They all think it's OK
because it's only a laugh and a joke
and they don't really mean it anyway
but Billy doesn't know that.

Billy doesn't know that
and because of that
Billy doesn't like school really.

The Magician's Composition of a Spell
of Great Precision

The magician with ambition was a mystical physician
who sought the composition of a spell of great precision.
For all things scientific
his knowledge was prolific:
voltage and transmission, gaseous ignition,
simple recognition of nuclear collision
and specific hieroglyphics was wicked and terrific.

This wizard of decision was a great mathematician,
a master statistician of addition and division.
For all things mathematical
his brain was acrobatical:
fractions and subtractions, factors and reactions,
equation complications, long multiplications,
computations problematical his mind was telepathical.

The solution's constitution was brought unto fruition,
magic spells and sorcery defying definition.
An amazing combination of enchanting calculations.
A wonderful creation beyond imagination.
A crazy composition of wish and superstition
fulfilling the ambition of this magician's vision
the lotions and the potions made him such a rich 'un
thanks to their transmission on national television.

Mum Used Prittstick

Mum used Prittstick
instead of lipstick
then went and kissed my dad.

Two days passed
both stuck fast
. . . the longest snog they ever had.

My Dad the Headmaster

My dad the Headmaster knows every single rule
and when he is at home he thinks that he's at school.
He rings the bell each morning and I'd better not be late
so I'm washed and down for breakfast at exactly ten to eight.

He stands and takes the register, checks my shirt and tie,
then he says 'Good Morning' and I have to reply
'Gerd mor-ning Far-ther' in that monotone drone
then hear his assembly in our very own home.

He has a list of rules that are pasted on each door:
No Spitting. No Chewing. No Litter On The Floor.
No Music. No Jewellery. No Make-Up. No Telly.
No Making Rude Noises Especially If They're Smelly.

No Videos. No Football. No Coloured Socks Or Laces.
No Trainers. No Jeans. No Smiling Faces.
No Sticking Bubble Gum In Your Sister's Hair.
No Wiping Bogies Down The Side Of The Chair.

He has a list of sayings for all types of occasion
and a set of phrases for every situation:
'Don't run down the stairs. Speak when spoken to.
Put your hand up first if you want to use the loo.'

'I don't mind how long I wait. Listen when I'm speaking.
No one leaves the table until we've finished eating.
Don't interrupt and don't answer back.
Don't do this and don't do that.'

Yes my dad the Headmaster knows every single rule
and when he is at home he thinks that he's at school.
But I am not the only one who does what he is told.
Dad never complains if his dinner is cold.

He's ever so polite when my mother is around
and mumbles 'Yes, my dear' while looking at the ground.
Her foghorn commands, they really drive him crazy.
Dad's scared stiff of Mum cos she's a dinner lady!

DO THE WASHING UP NOW!

YES, MY DEAR

Superman's Dog

Superman's dog – he's the best
Helping pets in distress
Red and gold pants and vest
'SD' on his chest

Superman's dog – X-ray sight
Green bones filled with Kryptonite
Bright blue lycra tights in flight
Faster than a meteorite

Better than Batman's Robin
Rougher than Robin's bat
Faster than Spiderman's spider
Cooler than Catwoman's cat

Superman's dog – bionic scent
Crime prevention – his intent
Woof and tough – cement he'll dent
What's his name – Bark Kent!

Wizard with the Ball

Young Arthur Merlin's spellbinding
His skills are crystal clear
A wizard with the ball
He makes it disappear!

Which is very useful in the opposition's penalty area.

Coolscorin' Matchwinnin' Celebratin' Striker!

I'm a shirt removin' crowd salutin'
handstandin' happy landin'
rockin' rollin' divin' slidin'
posin' poutin' loud shoutin'
pistol packin' smoke blowin'
flag wavin' kiss throwin'
hipswingin' armwavin'
breakdancin' cool ravin'
shoulder shruggin' team huggin'
hot shootin' rootin' tootin'
somersaultin' fence vaultin'
last minute goal grinnin'
shimmy shootin' shin spinnin'
celebratin' cup winnin' STRIKER!

ACKNOWLEDGEMENTS

Ian McMillan

'School in the Holidays', 'Out Of Season', 'Homework' and 'Another Christmas Present From Aunty Mabel' first published in *OK Gimme* by Versewagon Press; 'This Little Poem' first published in *The First Lick Of The Lolly* by Macmillan; 'Ten Things Found In A Wizard's Pocket' first published in *Wizard Poems* by Oxford University Press; 'Can't Be Bothered To Think Of A Title' first published in *New Angles* by Oxford University Press; 'Going To Sleep' first published in *Twinkle Twinkle Chocolate Bar* by Oxford University Press; 'Elephant Dreams' first published in *A Trunkful of Elephants* by Methuen; 'Coded Nursery Rhymes' first published in *My First Has Gone Bonkers* by Oxford University Press; 'The Fog and Me' first published in *Language in Colour* by Belain Publications; 'Goodnight Steven' first published in *Another Fourth Poetry Book* by Oxford University Press.

David Harmer

'There's A Monster In The Garden' first published in *Creaking Down The Corridor* by A Twist In The Tale Press; 'What Mountains Do' first published in *Another Third Poetry Book* Ed. John Foster by Oxford University Press; 'On A Blue Day' first published in *A Fifth Poetry Book* Ed. John Foster by Oxford University Press; 'It's Behind You' first published in *The Usborne Book of Scary Poems* Ed. Heather Amery by Usborne; 'The Elephant's Dictionary' first published in *A Trunkful of Elephants* Ed. Judith Nicholls by Methuen; 'Harry Hobgoblin's Superstore' first published in *Magic Poems* Ed. John Foster by Oxford University Press; 'Barry's Budgie – Beware!' first published in *Spill the Beans* by A Twist in the Tale Press.

Paul Cookson

'Sea Shoals See Shows On The Sea Bed' first published in *Spill the Beans* by A Twist in the Tale; 'At the Back of The Cupboard Under The Stairs', 'An Elephant's Nose is Long I Suppose' first published in *Rhyming Rhythms for Twisted Tongues* by A Twist In The Tale; 'L Plates On My Football Shirt', 'The Toilet Seat Has Teeth', 'Mother Is A Skinhead', first published in *The Toilet Seat Has Teeth* by A Twist In The Tale; 'Billy Doesn't Like School Really', 'Mum For A Day', 'It' first published in *The Amazing Captain Concorde* by A Twist In The Tale; 'Mum Used Prittstick' first published in *Happy As A Pig In Muck* by A Twist In The Tale.

A selected list of poetry books available from Macmillan

The prices shown below are correct at the time of going to press. However, Macmillan Publishers reserve the right to show new retail prices on covers which may differ from those previously advertised.

The Secret Lives of Teachers
Revealing rhymes, chosen by Brian Moses
0 330 34265 7
£3.50

'Ere we Go!
Football poems, chosen by David Orme
0 330 32986 3
£2.99

You'll Never Walk Alone
More football poems, chosen by David Orme
0 330 33787 4
£2.99

Nothing Tastes Quite Like a Gerbil
And other vile verses, chosen by David Orme
0 330 34632 6
£2.99

Custard Pie
Poems that are jokes, chosen by Pie Corbett
0 330 33992 3
£2.99

Parent-Free Zone
Poems about parents, chosen by Brian Moses
0 330 34554 0
£2.99

Tongue Twisters and Tonsil Twizzlers
Poems chosen by Paul Cookson
0 330 34941 4
£2.99

All Macmillan titles can be ordered at your local bookshop or are available by post from:

**Book Service by Post
PO Box 29, Douglas, Isle of Man IM99 1BQ**

Credit cards accepted. For details:
Telephone: 01624 675137
Fax: 01624 670923
E-mail: bookshop@enterprise.net

Free postage and packing in the UK.
Overseas customers: add £1 per book (paperback)
and £3 per book (hardback).